World of Bugs
WEIRD WALKING STICKS

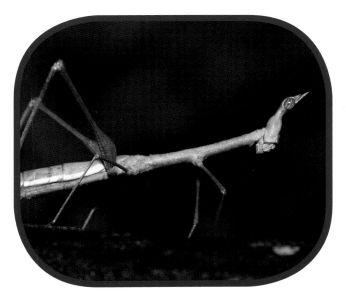

By Greg Roza

Gareth Stevens
Publishing

Please visit our Web site, www.garethstevens.com. For a free color catalog of all our high-quality books, call toll free 1-800-542-2595 or fax 1-877-542-2596.

Library of Congress Cataloging-in-Publication Data

Roza, Greg.
 Weird walking sticks / Greg Roza.
     p. cm. — (World of bugs)
  ISBN 978-1-4339-4616-5 (pbk.)
  ISBN 978-1-4339-4617-2 (6-pack)
  ISBN 978-1-4339-4615-8 (library binding)
 1. Stick insects—Juvenile literature. I. Title.
  QL509.5.R69 2011
  595.7'29—dc22

                                    2010031815

First Edition

Published in 2011 by
Gareth Stevens Publishing
111 East 14th Street, Suite 349
New York, NY 10003

Copyright © 2011 Gareth Stevens Publishing

Editor: Greg Roza
Designer: Christopher Logan

Photo credits: Cover, pp. 1, 3, 5, 9, 11, 13, 15, 17, 23, 24 (all) Shutterstock.com; pp. 7, 19 iStockphoto.com; p. 21 Jupiterimages/Photos.com/Thinkstock.

Printed in the United States of America

CPSIA compliance information: Batch #CW11GS: For further information contact Gareth Stevens, New York, New York at 1-800-542-2595.

WEIRD
WALKING STICKS

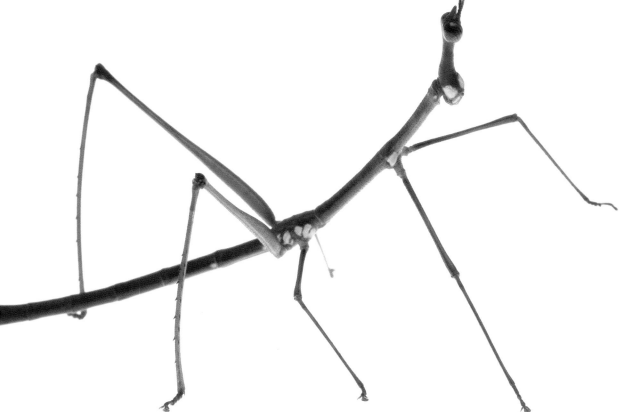

A walking stick is a bug.
It looks like a stick.

A walking stick hides in a tree.

7

Most stick bugs do not have wings.

This walking stick looks like a leaf. It is called a leaf bug.

11

Leaf bugs have wings.

13

A walking stick has six legs.

15

A walking stick has two feelers.

A walking stick eats leaves.

A walking stick lays eggs on the ground.

Walking stick eggs look like seeds.

23

Words to Know

eggs

feeler

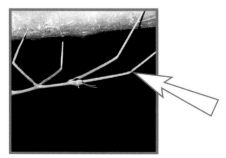

leg

wing